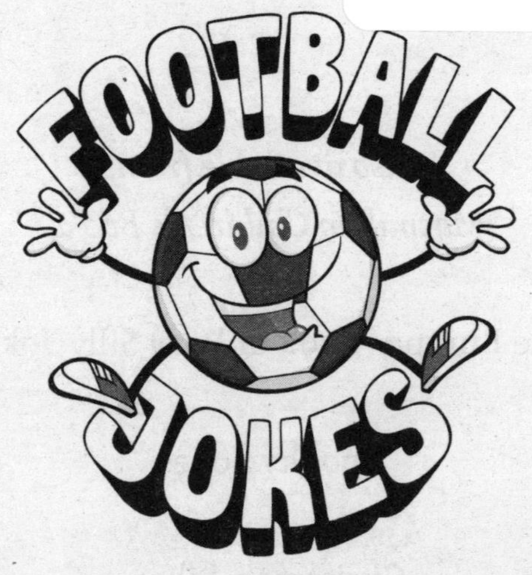

Knock, knock . . .
Who's there?
Jane.
Jane who?
Jane who did the
drawings in this book.

(That's Jane Eccles, who loves drawing
and works in a tiny room in her house
in Hampshire, where she lives with her
husband and son and small grey cat.)

FOOTBALL JOKES

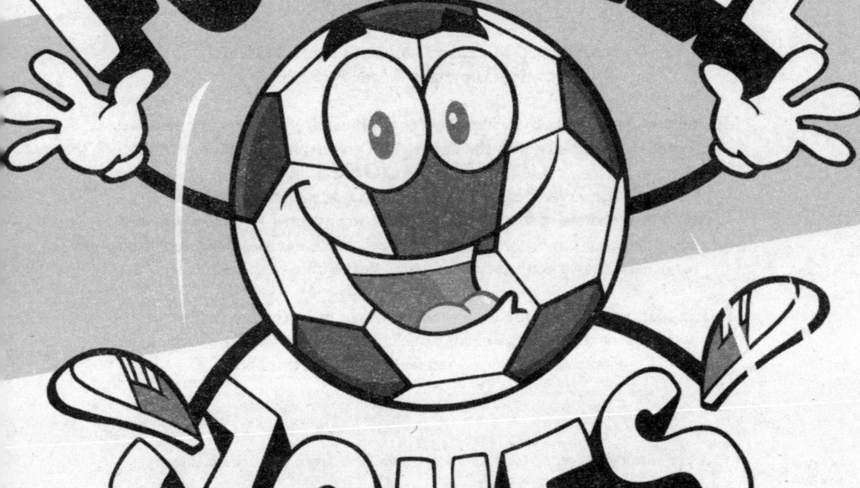

Illustrated by Jane Eccles

*For Theo, who prefers rugby to football,
but will like the critters in this book*

First published 2014 by Macmillan Children's Books, an imprint of Pan Macmillan

This edition published 2026 by Rocket Fox,
an imprint of Pan Macmillan
The Smithson, 6 Briset Street, London EC1M 5NR
EU representative: Macmillan Publishers Ireland Ltd, 1st Floor,
The Liffey Trust Centre, 117–126 Sheriff Street Upper, Dublin 1 D01 YC43
Associated companies throughout the world

ISBN 978-1-0374-0062-9

Text copyright © Macmillan Children's Books 2014, 2026
Illustrations copyright © Jane Eccles 2014

The right of Jane Eccles to be identified as the illustrator of this work has been
asserted in accordance with the Copyright, Designs and Patents Act 1988.

1 3 5 7 9 8 6 4 2

A CIP catalogue record for this book is available from the British Library.

Printed and bound in the UK using 100% Renewable Electricity by CPI Group (UK) Ltd

Visit **www.panmacmillan.com** to read more about all our books and to buy them.

Contents

Kick-Off

What can light up a dull evening?
A football match.

What goes stomp, stomp, stomp, squelch?
An elephant with wet football boots.

DAD: How did this window get broken?

TOMMY: Er, my football took a shot at goal while I was cleaning it.

Young Alec came off the pitch looking very dejected and slunk into the dressing room.

'I've never played so badly before,' he sighed.

'Oh,' answered a fellow player. 'You've played before, have you?'

TEACHER: And why were you late for school today, Lily?

LILY: I was dreaming about a football match and they went into extra time.

A tourist visiting London stopped a man carrying a football and asked, 'How do I get to Wembley?' 'Practice,' was the reply.

How can you stop moles digging
up the football pitch?
Hide their spades.

FATHER MONSTER: Why don't you go out
and play football with your little brother?
LITTLE MONSTER: Oh, Dad, I'd much rather
play with a real football.

Why was the mummy no good at football?
He was too wrapped up in himself.

What did the pitch say to the player?
'I hate it when people treat me like dirt.'

What's the difference between the
Prince of Wales and a throw-in?
*One's heir to the throne; the other's
thrown to the air.*

MOTHER: David! It's time to get up! It's 8.15!

DAVID: Who's winning?

Why is Mary Earps the richest
player out of the Lionesses?
She's great at saving.

When is a footballer like
a grandfather clock?
When they're a striker.

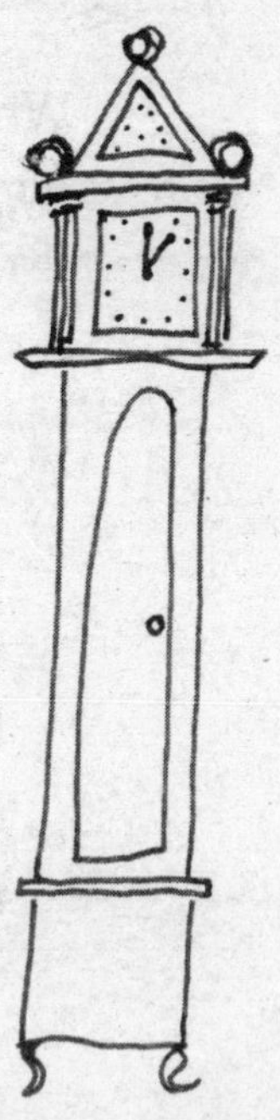

When are footballers like babies?
When they dribble.

When is a kick like a boat?
When it's a punt.

What happened when
the male footballer married
a female footballer?
*People said it was
a perfect match.*

How do you stop a hot
and sweaty footballer
from smelling?

Put a peg on his nose.

What's large, grey and carries a
trunk and two pairs of football boots?

An elephant that's just joined the team.

What do you do if you're too
hot at a football match?

Sit next to a fan.

What did the ball say to the footballer?
'I get a kick out of you.'

Why did Cole Palmer wear a coat
on the pitch at the Euros?
He was too cold.

Why are there fouls in football?
Same reason there are ducks in cricket.

KEN: I've just been to the doctor and
they said I can't play football.
BEN: Oh? When did they see you play?

Why can't horses play football?
Because they've got two left feet.

What is the best way to protect
your house from bad football?
A Guard-iola dog.

What kind of tea does Alex Morgan drink?
Penaltea.

The doctor was giving
members of the team a
medical.

'Breathe out three times,'
he said to one of the
players.

'Are you checking my
lungs?' asked the player.

'No, I'm going to clean
my spectacles,' replied
the doctor.

How can a footballer stop
their nose running?

Put out a foot and trip it up.

How does an
octopus go onto
a football pitch?
Well-armed!

Why was the centipede no use
to the football team?
*He never arrived on the pitch until half-time –
it took him so long to lace up his boots.*

Which animal plays
football standing on
its head?
Yoga Bear.

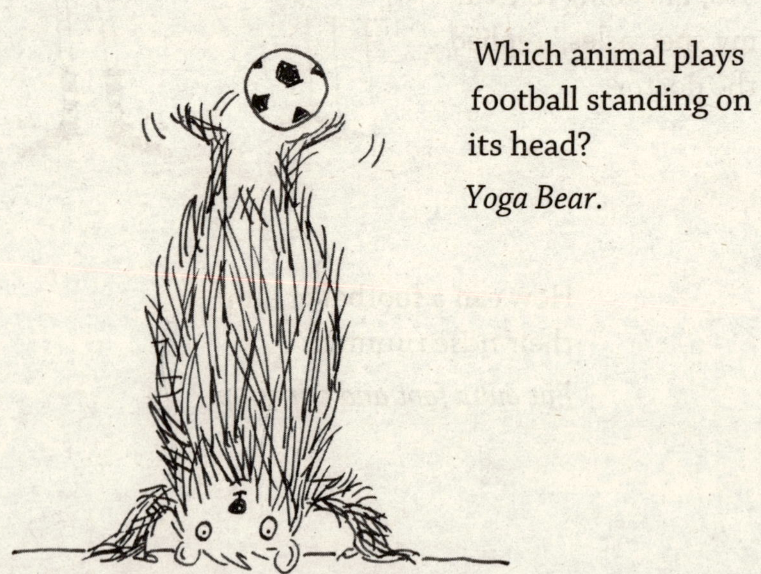

What two things should a footballer never
eat before breakfast?

Lunch and dinner.

What's black and white
and wears dark glasses?

A football in disguise.

What happens
to the boy who
misses the bus
home from the
match?

*He catches it when he
gets home.*

Two flies were playing football in a saucer.
One said to the other, 'We'll have to do better
than this – we're playing in the cup next week!'

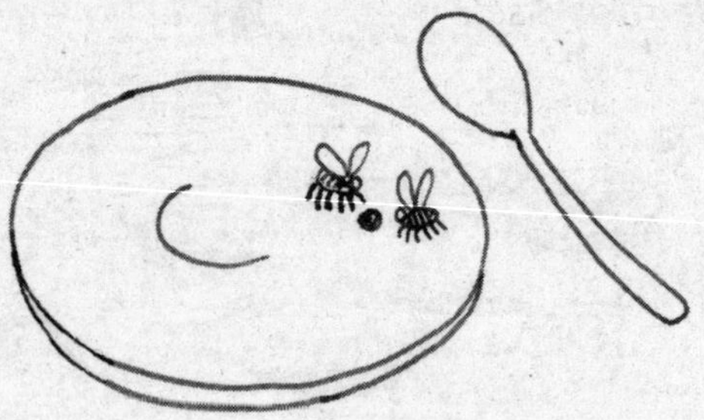

What happened when a herd of
cows had a football match?
There was udder chaos.

What can a footballer never make right?
Their left foot.

How do ghost footballers keep fit?
With regular exorcise.

What's the difference between a flea-ridden
dog and a bored football spectator?
One's going to itch; the other's itching to go.

What has two feet like
a footballer, two eyes
like a footballer and two
arms like a footballer,
yet isn't a footballer?

*A photograph of a
footballer.*

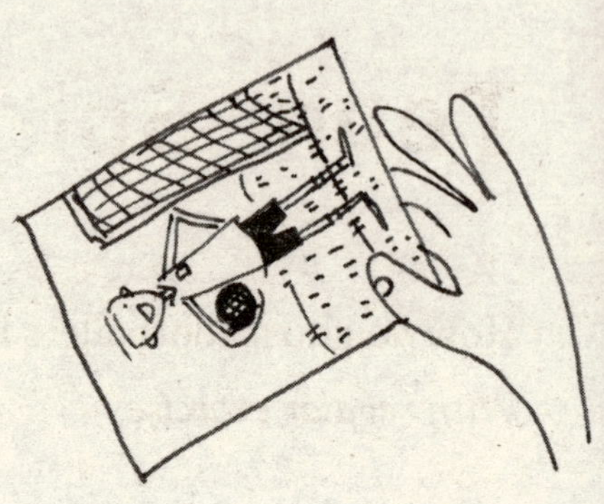

How do you hire a
professional footballer?

Stand them on a chair.

Team Spirit

Which football team never
meets before a match?
Queen's Park Strangers.

Which football team
should you not eat
in a sandwich?
Oldham.

GILL: My dog can play football.

BILL: Really? What a clever animal!

GILL: Oh, I don't know. When he plays
for the local team it usually loses.

LENNY: The Leeds manager said I'd make
a great footballer if it weren't for two things.

BENNY: What were they?

LENNY: My feet.

MR GREEN: I've been invited to join the firm's football team. They want me to play for them very badly.

MR BROWN: In that case, you're just the man.

Manchester United was playing Chelsea at Stamford Bridge. A man wearing a bright red-and-white rosette walked up to the ticket office and asked the price of admission.

'Twenty pounds, sir,' said the attendant.

'Here's ten pounds,' replied the man. 'There's only one team worth watching.'

SCOTTISH TEAM CAPTAIN: How can
we raise the level of our game?

SCOTTISH TEAM MANAGER: Play at
the top of Ben Nevis?

What's yellow, has twenty-two
legs and peels off at half-time?
Banana United.

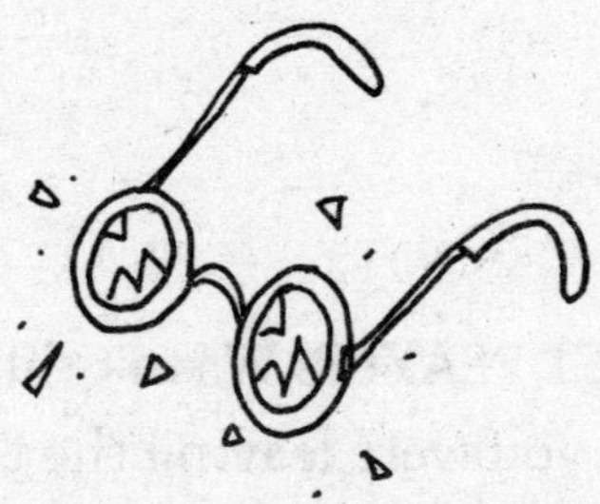

After the match the team was in the dressing-room when the trainer came in and asked if anyone had seen her spectacles.

'Yes,' replied one of the players. 'They were out on the pitch.'

'Then why didn't you bring them in?' asked the trainer.

'I didn't think you'd want them after everyone had trodden on them,' replied the player.

The architect was showing the team round the new stadium.

'I think you'll find it hasn't got a flaw,' he said proudly.

'What do we walk on then?' asked one of the players.

FIRST PLAYER: Wasn't the captain angry when you said you were leaving the team next month?

SECOND PLAYER: Yes. He thought it was this month.

Which member of
the team flies
down the field?
The winger.

Why did the potato
go to the match?
*So it could root for
the home team.*

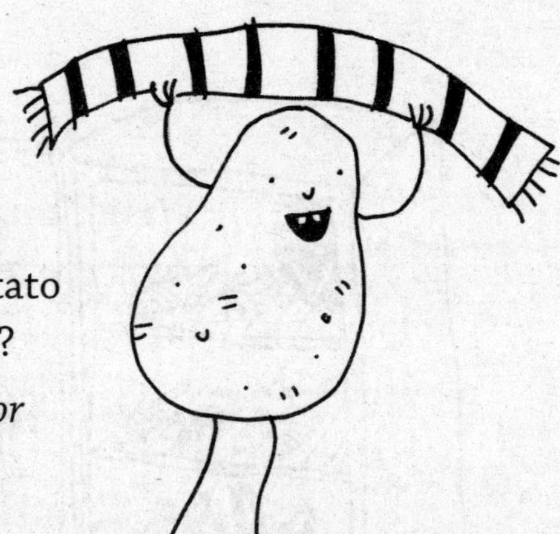

What position did the ducks
play in the football team?
Right and left quack.

Which football team comes
out of an ice-cream van?
Aston Vanilla.

Which London team keeps its boots in the fridge?
Tottenham Coldspur.

Which football team spends all
its spare time at music events?
Blackburn Ravers.

MR ROUND: I hear your son has a place in the
school football team. What position does he play?
MR LONG: I think he's one of the drawbacks.

A man went to meet the members of a vegetable football team.

'This stick of celery is our goalie, the carrots are our centre forwards and the onions are our backs,' explained his host.

'And what's that one over there, telling everyone else what to do?' the man asked, pointing to a mud-covered vegetable that was lounging around.

'Oh, him?' replied the host. 'He's our coach potato.'

A man was up in court charged with trying to set fire to Chelsea's grandstand.

When questioned by the judge he said he had a burning interest in football.

What team is good in an omelette?
Best Ham.

Which Midlands team shrank and
became known as the clump of trees?
Notts Forest.

What was the monkey in the
team especially good at?
Banana shots.

FIRST PLAYER: Why did you call
the team captain Camera?

SECOND PLAYER: Because they
are always snapping at me.

If it takes twenty people six months to build
a grandstand at the football pitch, how long
would it take forty people to build it?

*No time at all, because the twenty people had
already completed it!*

Why is Lionel Messi like a magician?
He has loads of hat tricks.

When Harry retired
from the team he said
he was going to work
in a bank.

'Why do you want to do
that?' asked Beth.

'I've heard there's money
in it,' replied Harry.

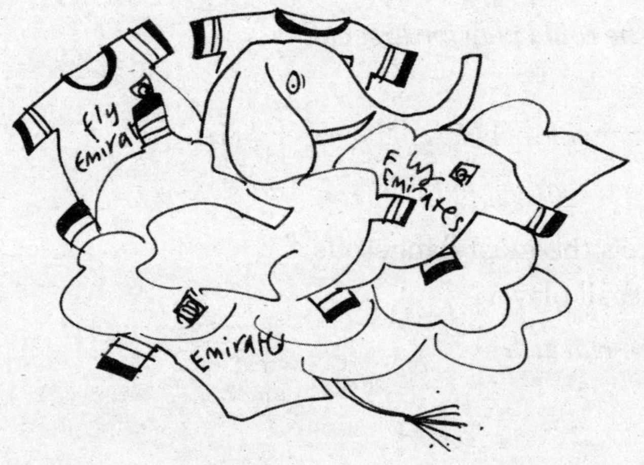

MANAGER: This dressing room is disgusting!
It hasn't been cleaned for a month!

CLEANER: Don't blame me. I've only been
here for a fortnight.

Why did the elephant paint his toenails red?

So he could hide in a pile of Arsenal shirts.

Why did the elephant wear a red-and-white shirt?
So she could play for Arsenal.

Who's the most dangerous
football player?
Eden Hazard.

What do you call a
noisy football fan?
A foot-bawler.

Why did the manager have the pitch flooded?
She wanted to bring her sub.

What's healthy and
scores lots of goals?
Fruit Salah-d.

What happened when the
footballer went to see his doctor
to complain about flat feet?
The doctor gave him a bicycle pump.

Who was the sheep's favourite footballer?
Paul Pog-BAAA.

I was wondering why the football
kept getting bigger and bigger . . .
And then it hit me!

What goes in pink and comes out blue?
*A footballer who plays for a team that
only has cold showers.*

DANIEL: While Darren was taking a
shower after the match, someone
stole all his clothes.

TRACEY: Oh dear! What
did he come home in?

DANIEL: The dark!

TALENT SCOUT: Your number six looks
as if he might be a good footballer if his
legs weren't so short.

TEAM MANAGER: They're not that
short. They do both reach the floor.

Why did the footballer
put her bed in the
fireplace?

*She wanted to sleep
like a log.*

Knock, Knock on the Dressing-Room Door

Knock, knock.

Who's there?

Aladdin.

Aladdin who?

Aladdin the street's waiting for
you to come out and play football.

Knock, knock.
Who's there?
Alison.
Alison who?
Alison to the football results
on the radio.

Knock, knock.
Who's there?
Euripides.
Euripides who?
Euripides football shorts and
you buy me a new pair.

Knock, knock.
Who's there?
Godfrey.
Godfrey who?
Godfrey tickets for the
match on Saturday.

Knock, knock.
Who's there?
Kerry.
Kerry who?
Kerry me off the pitch –
I think my leg's broken.

Knock, knock.
Who's there?
Juno.
Juno who?
Juno what time the kick-off is?

Knock, knock.

Who's there?

Al B.

Al B who?

Al B home straight after the match.

Knock, knock.

Who's there?

Howell.

Howell who?

Howell you take
that corner?

Knock, knock.
Who's there?
Weed.
Weed who?
Weed like to win this game.

Knock, knock.
Who's there?
Ammonia.
Ammonia who?
Ammonia little boy and
I can't run as fast as you.

Knock, knock.

Who's there?

Ida.

Ida who?

Ida terrible time getting to the match –
all the buses were full.

Knock, knock.

Who's there?

Money.

Money who?

Money hurts since I
twisted it on the pitch.

Knock, knock.
Who's there?
Harvey.
Harvey who?
Harvey going to have another
game before lunch?

Knock, knock.
Who's there?
Stu.
Stu who?
Stu late to score a goal now.

Knock, knock.

Who's there?

Waiter.

Waiter who?

Waiter minute
while I tie my
bootlaces.

Knock, knock.

Who's there?

Luke.

Luke who?

Luke, he's just scored a goal.

Knock, knock.
Who's there?
Oily.
Oily who?
Oily in the morning's the best time to train.

Knock, knock.
Who's there?
Saul.
Saul who?
Saul over when the final whistle blows.

Knock, knock.

Who's there?

Argo.

Argo who?

Argo to Elland Road
on Saturdays.

Knock, knock.

Who's there?

General Lee.

General Lee who?

General Lee I support Chelsea but
today I'm rooting for Fulham.

Knock, knock.

Who's there?

Farmer.

Farmer who?

Farmer birthday I got a
new pair of football boots.

Knock, knock.

Who's there?

Nana.

Nana who?

Nana your business who we put in goal.

Knock, knock.

Who's there?

Ken.

Ken who?

Ken Harry come out
and play football?

Knock, knock.

Who's there?

Hurd.

Hurd who?

Hurd my foot so I
couldn't play today.

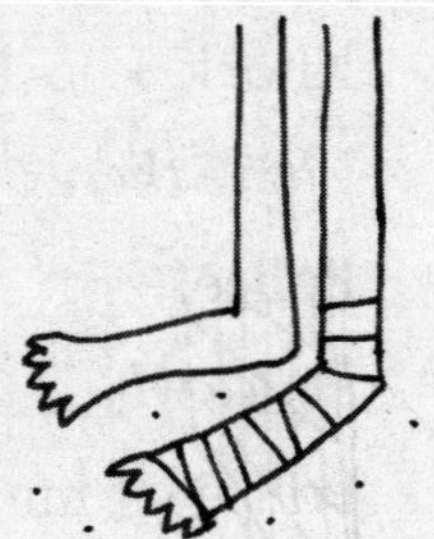

Knock, knock.

Who's there?

Scold.

Scold who?

Scold wearing shorts to play football in winter.

Knock, knock.

Who's there?

Police.

Police who?

Police let me play with your new football.

Knock, knock.

Who's there?

Ammon.

Ammon who?

Ammon awfully good football player. Can I be in your team?

Knock, knock.

Who's there?

Omar.

Omar who?

Omar goodness, what a shot!

Knock, knock.
Who's there?
Macho.
Macho who?
Macho the Day.

Knock, knock.
Who's there?
Wanda.
Wanda who?
Wanda buy a new football?

Knock, knock.

Who's there?

Aardvark.

Aardvark who?

Aardvark to Scotland to see Celtic play.

Knock, knock.

Who's there?

Dozen.

Dozen who?

Dozen anyone in this village play football?

Knock, knock.

Who's there?

Gladys.

Gladys who?

Gladys Saturday – we can go to the match.

Knock, knock.

Who's there?

Stan.

Stan who?

Stan back – I'm going to shoot!

Knock, knock.
Who's there?
Philippa.
Philippa who?
Philippa bathtub –
I'm covered in mud.

Knock, knock.
Who's there?
Willy.
Willy who?
Willy score? Bet he won't!

Knock, knock.

Who's there?

Wayne.

Wayne who?

Wayne never stops when
I play football.

Knock, knock.

Who's there?

Snow.

Snow who?

Snow use, I'm going to
give you a red card.

Knock, knock.
Who's there?
Norma Lee.
Norma Lee who?
Norma Lee I play in goal but
today I'm at left back.

Knock, knock.
Who's there?
Althea.
Althea who?
Althea later,
down the club.

Knock, knock.
Who's there?
Buster.
Buster who?
Buster Old Trafford, please.

Knock, knock.
Who's there?
Ivan.
Ivan who?
Ivan new pair of boots – do you like them?

Knock, knock.
Who's there?
Ben.
Ben who?
Ben playing football today, have you?

Knock, knock.

Who's there?

Yolande.

Yolande who?

Yolande me some
money to get into
the match and I'll pay
you back next week.

Knock, knock.

Who's there?

Mister.

Mister who?

Mister bus, that's why
I'm late for the match.

Knock, knock.

Who's there?

Anna.

Anna who?

Anna rack keeps you warm after football.

Knock, knock.

Who's there?

Hammond.

Hammond who?

Hammond eggs are great after
football.

Knock, knock.

Who's there?

Harriet.

Harriet who?

Harriet all my sandwiches –
now I'm too weak to play!

Half-Time

Take a quick break from the golden game to catch up on your reading. Here are some of the titles in the club library.

Embarrassing Moments
on the Pitch *by Lucy Lastic*

Twenty-five Years in Goal
by Annie Versary

Will He Win?
by Betty Wont

Let the Game Begin
by Sally Forth

The Unhappy Fan
by Mona Lott

The Poor Striker
by Miss D. Goal

Why I Gave Up Football *by Arthur Itis*

Keep Trying Until the Final Whistle *by Percy Vere*

Heading the Ball *by I. C. Starrs*

We'll Win the Cup *by R. U. Sure*

Pre-Match-Night Nerves
by Eliza Wake

Keep Your Subs Handy
by Justin Case

Training Hard
by Xavier Strength

Buying Good Players
by Ivor Fortune

The New Player
by Izzy Anygood

Great Shot!
by Major Runn

Advertising the Match *by Bill Poster*

What do you cheer at
the Women's World Cup?
Megan Rapin-GO.

What reaches 100mph and
always scores?

A Harrykane.

A young football fan from Quebec
Once wrapped both his feet round
His neck.
Though he tried hard, he got
Tied up in a knot,
And now he's an absolute wreck.

DAD: Your school report is terrible. You've come bottom out of twenty in every subject. You're even bottom in football – and that's your favourite.

SON: It could be worse.

DAD: How?

SON: I'd be bottom out of thirty if I was in Katie's class. It's bigger.

A young football fan of Southend
Wrote in rhyme – several verses she penned,
Of their triumphs and glory,
Their total history –
It drove all her friends round the bend.

What's the best day for a footballer
to eat bacon and eggs for breakfast?
Fry-day.

Why did the footballer's dog
run away from home?
Doggone if I know!

ERIC: My doctor says I can't play football.
DEREK: Oh, so she's seen you play too, has she?

Why did the man become a marathon
runner instead of a footballer?

The doctor told him he had athlete's foot.

Why did the footballer
call her dog Carpenter?

*He was always doing little
jobs around the house.*

Two girls were walking past a house surrounded
by a high wall when the owner came out holding
a football. 'Is this your ball?' he demanded.
'Er, has it done any damage?' asked the first girl.
'No,' said the householder.
'Then it's ours,' said the second girl.

What position did Cinderella
play in the football team?
Sweeper.

Why was Cinderella thrown
out of the football team?
*Because she kept running
away from the ball.*

What is a goalkeeper's
favourite snack?

Beans on post.

How do chickens encourage
their football teams?

They egg them on.

What insect doesn't play
football well?

The fumble bee.

My dad was renowned for 'thinking outside of the box'. Great man, but a terrible goalkeeper.

BOSS: I thought you wanted the afternoon off to see your dentist.

MR BROWN: That's right.

BOSS: Then how come I saw you leaving the football ground with a friend?

MR BROWN: That was my dentist.

MUM: And was there a fight at the match again? You've lost your front teeth.

TOMMY: No I haven't. They're in my pocket.

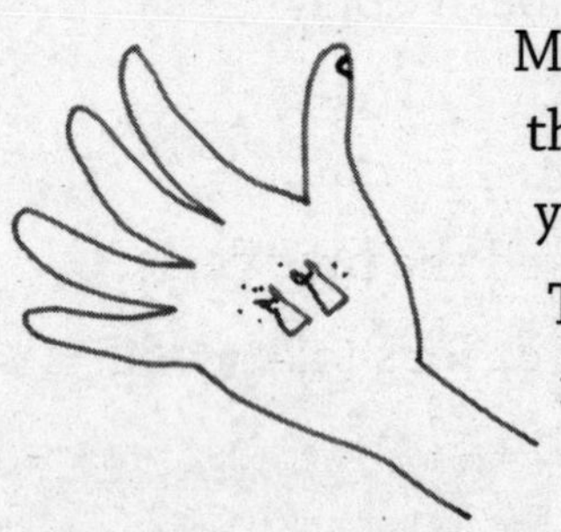

My girlfriend is the star goalie of her
local football team . . . she's a keeper.

Two fleas were leaving a football
match when it started to rain.
'Shall we walk?' asked the first flea.
'No,' said the second, 'let's take a dog.'

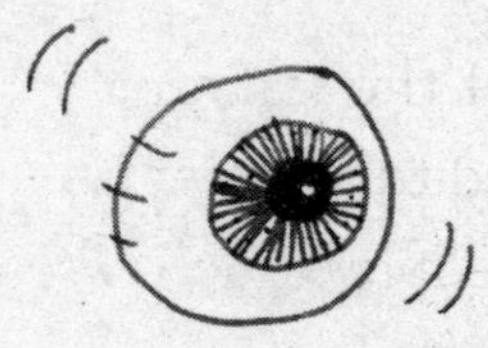

How can you tell when a footballer has a glass eye?

When it comes out in conversation.

It was Christmas time, and a little girl was being asked by her teacher about the Three Wise Men.

'Who were they?' asked the teacher.

'They were footballers,' replied the little girl.

'Whatever do you mean?' asked the teacher.

'Well, the carol says, "We three kings of Orient are . . ."'

LEN: Did you hear about the Italian footballer who belonged to a secret society that beat people up with shopping baskets?

KEN: No!

LEN: Yes. He was a member of the Raffia.

FIRST FOOTBALLER: Did you enjoy your massage?

SECOND FOOTBALLER: Oh yes. I like to feel kneaded.

Why did the doctor write on the footballer's toes?

To add a footnote.

Which footballer can jump higher than a house?

All of them – houses can't jump.

What was wrong with the footballer
whose nose ran and feet smelt?

They were built upside down.

FOOTBALLER: I've a terrible pain in
my right foot. What should I do?

PHYSIOTHERAPIST: Kick the ball
with your left foot.

PARK-KEEPER: Why are you boys
playing football in the trees?

RASHID AND MO: Because the sign says
no ball games on the grass.

Why do ghosts play football?
For the ghouls, of course.

Which player uses a fridge wisely?
Ben Chilwell.

Did you hear the story of the
peacock who played football?
It was a beautiful tail.

Own Goal

FIRST FOOTBALLER: How did you manage to break your leg?

SECOND FOOTBALLER: See those steps down to the car park?

FIRST FOOTBALLER: Yes.

SECOND FOOTBALLER: I didn't.

Who is the funniest football player?
Erling Ha-Ha-Land.

ELLA: I'm sorry I missed the goal.
I could kick myself, I really could.

BELLA: Don't bother – you'd miss.

It was a cold, wet, miserable day and the
goalie had had a bad match, allowing
several goals through. As he sat moping
in the dressing room, he sniffed and
muttered, 'I think I've caught a cold.'

'Thank goodness you can catch something,'
said the captain.

What gloves can a goalie see
and smell but not wear?
Foxgloves.

The goalie was so short-sighted she couldn't see the
ball until it was too late. A doctor friend prescribed
carrots to help her eyesight. The goalie ate lots of
carrots, but went back to the doctor a week later,
saying she still couldn't catch the ball because
every time she ran she now tripped over her ears.

What's the difference between a gutter
and a poor goalie?

One catches drops; the other drops catches.

Which football team has
nailed their formation?

The Hammers.

Did you hear about the player who threw away his boots because he thought they were sticking out their tongues at him?

Why did the man come onto the pitch dressed in diving gear?

He'd been told he might be needed as a sub.

PE TEACHER: Now, Billy, you promised to practise hard at your football, didn't you?

BILLY: Yes.

PE TEACHER: And I promised to put you in detention if you didn't practise?

BILLY: Yes. But I don't mind if you break your promise.

GOALIE: Where shall we put the new player?

CAPTAIN: What's his name?

GOALIE: Robin Swallow.

CAPTAIN: Put him on the wing.

Why didn't the dog want to play football?

Because he was a boxer.

Why can't you play football in the jungle?

Because there are too many cheetahs.

Why was the chicken sent off?
For persistent fowl play.

Who scored the most goals in the
Greek Mythology League?
The centaur forward.

Nobody ever passed the ball to Willy and
he was moaning in the dressing room that
he might as well be invisible.

'Who said that?' asked the captain.

What is black and white and black and white
and black and white?

A Newcastle United fan rolling down a hill.

Two young footballers were talking about the
illnesses and accidents they had had.

'Once I couldn't walk for a year,' said the first.

'When was that?' asked the other.

'When I was a baby,' replied the first.

Old Harry had been retired from the game for many years, but he still liked to tell people how good he'd once been.

'They still remember me, you know,' he said. 'Only yesterday, when I was at the players' entrance, there were lots of press photographers queuing to take my picture.'

'Really?' said a disbelieving listener.

'Yes. And if you don't believe me, ask David Beckham – he was standing next to me.'

The great goalkeeper Jim 'Big Hands'
O'Reilly was walking down the street.

'I recognize that man,' said Ken. 'But
what's his name?'

'That's Big Hands,' replied Ben.

'Oh, really?'

'No, O'Reilly.'

Who's in goal when the ghost
team plays football?
The ghoulie, of course!

My sister plays football for a team called the Musketeers. They've started the season well with three wins and a draw, all 4–1 and one 4 all.

ANGRY NEIGHBOUR: Didn't you hear me banging on your wall last night?

NEIGHBOUR: No, but don't worry – we had a bit of a party after the match and were making quite a lot of noise ourselves.

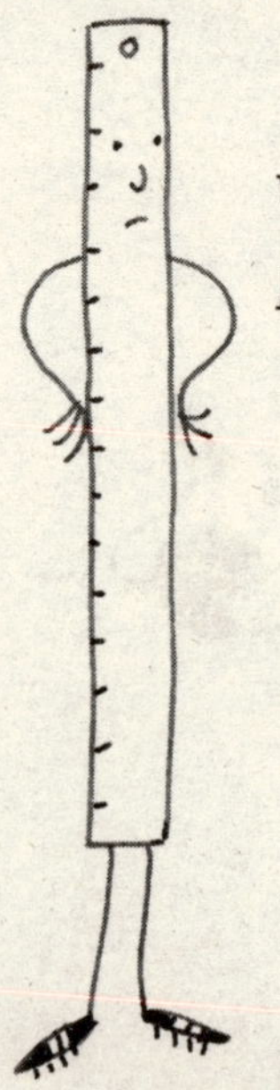

Why was the ruler no good at football?
He just didn't measure up.

DARREN: Did you hear about the
footballer who ate little bits of
metal all day?

SHARON: No.

DARREN: It was his staple diet.

Who is the slipperiest footballer
on the planet?

Antoine Grease-man.

WAYNE: Why didn't you set a knife and fork for
your brother when you laid the table?

JANE: Because Mum said that when he's been
playing football he eats like a horse.

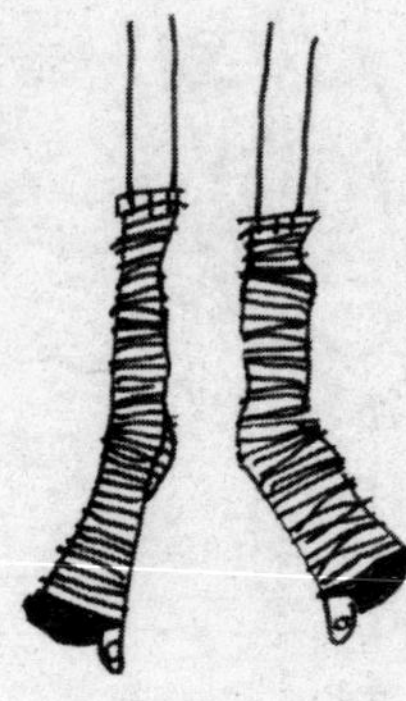

DAVINA: Mum, can I go out and play?

MUM: What, with those holes in your socks?

DAVINA: No, with Billy next door, he's got a new football.

Who ran out on the pitch when a player was injured and said, 'Miaow'?

The first aid kit.

Kitbag

What did the left football boot say to the right football boot?

'Between us we should have a ball.'

Who wears the biggest boots in the English team?

The player with the biggest feet.

Why don't grasshoppers watch football?
They prefer cricket!

What do jelly babies
wear on their feet when
they play football?
Gumboots.

MUM: You've got your boots on the wrong feet.
ALEC: But, Mum, these are the only feet I've got.

Which football team is the chewiest?
The Toffees.

What's the difference between an oak tree
and a tight football boot?

One makes acorns, the other makes corns ache.

DORIS: Did you hear the joke
about the dirty football shirt?

BORIS: No.

DORIS: That's one on you!

LITTLE TOMMY: I've looked everywhere for
my football boots and I can't find them.

TEACHER: Are you sure these aren't yours?
They're the only pair left.

LITTLE TOMMY: Quite sure. Mine had snow
on them.

MICKY: My sister's away training to be in a football team.

NICKY: Lucky thing! She must be quite grown up now.

MICKY: Yes. She wrote to us the other day saying she'd grown another foot, so my mum is knitting her an extra sock.

ANNA: Do you have holes in your football shorts?

BERTIE: No.

ANNA: Then how do you get them on?

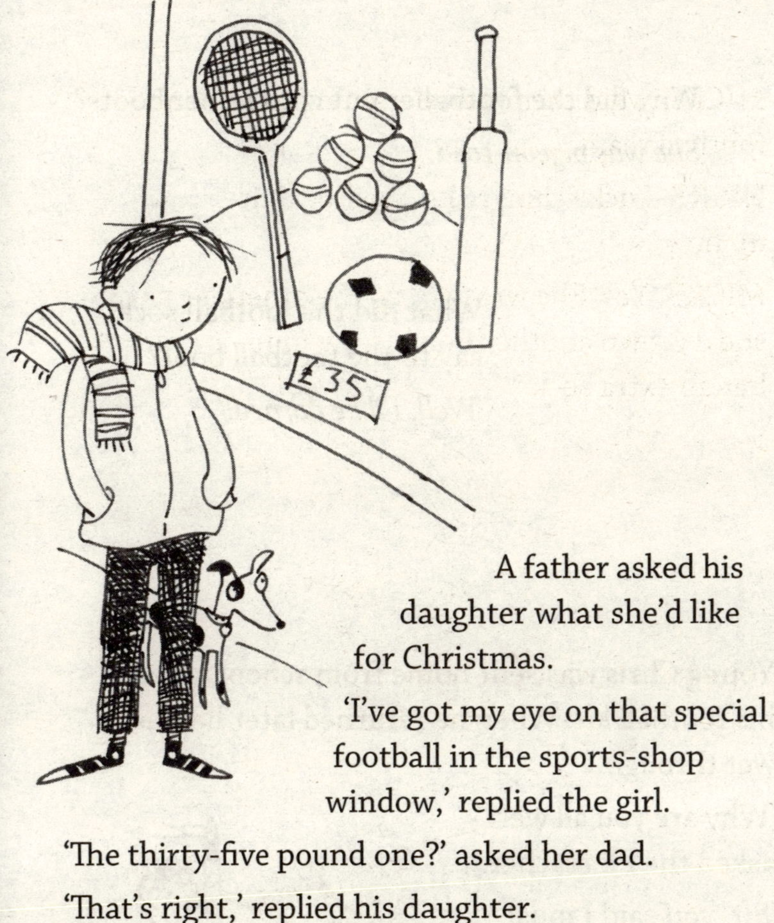

A father asked his
daughter what she'd like
for Christmas.

'I've got my eye on that special
football in the sports-shop
window,' replied the girl.

'The thirty-five pound one?' asked her dad.

'That's right,' replied his daughter.

'You'd better keep your eye on it then, cos it's
unlikely your boot will ever kick it,' said her dad
firmly.

What wears out football
boots but has no feet?
The ground.

Why did the footballer put corn in her boots?
She was pigeon-toed.

What did the football sock
say to the football boot?
'Well, I'll be darned!'

Young Chris was sent home from school to fetch
his football kit. When he returned later he was
wet through.

'Why are you all wet?'
asked the PE teacher.

'Sir, you said I must
go home to get my
kit, but it was in
the wash.'

FIRST SPIDER: I don't know what
to get my husband for Christmas.

SECOND SPIDER: Give him what
I gave mine – four pairs of football
boots.

Why does a professional footballer
always put his right boot on first?

*It would be silly to put the wrong boot on,
wouldn't it?*

FIRST FOOTBALLER: Do you think it
will rain for the match this afternoon?

SECOND FOOTBALLER: That
depends on the weather,
doesn't it?

OLDER BROTHER: Have
you got your football
boots on yet?

YOUNGER BROTHER:
Yes, all but one.

What does a footballer part
with but never give away?
His comb!

Why can't pigs play football?
Because they hog the ball.

CAPTAIN (looking at their watch): You should have been here at nine thirty.

LATE PLAYER: Why, what happened?

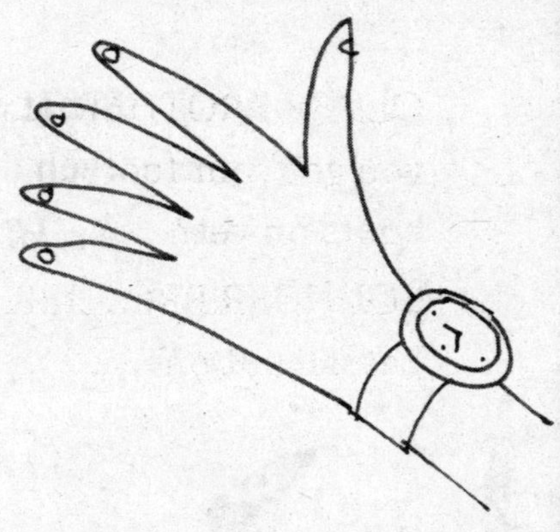

What runs around all day and lies at night with its tongue hanging out?

A football boot.

Two fans were discussing their packed lunches.

'What have you got?' asked Olli.

'Tongue sandwiches,' Eddie replied.

'Ugh, I couldn't eat something that had come out of an animal's mouth,' said Olli.

'What have you got then?' asked Eddie.

'Egg sandwiches.'

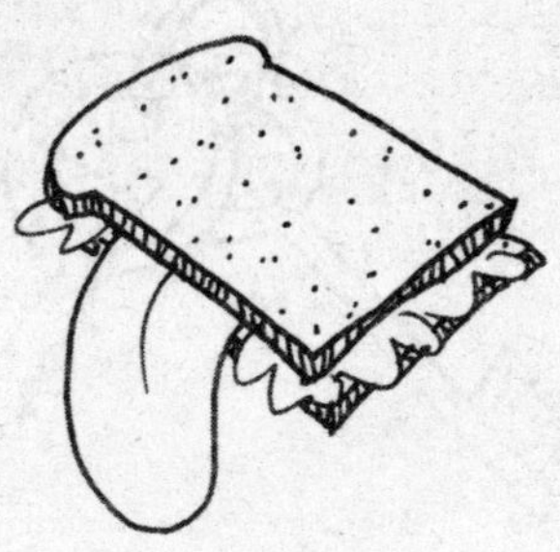

What can a footballer keep
even if he does give it away?
A cold!

INSURANCE AGENT: This is a very good policy, sir. We pay up to £1,000 for broken arms and legs.

CONFUSED FOOTBALLER: But what do you do with them all?

Why did the footballer stand on her head?
She was turning things over in her mind.

Why did the bald footballer throw away his keys?
He'd lost all his locks.

Why was the snowman no good
playing in the big match?
He got cold feet.

Why did the player throw a bucket of water
on the pitch when she made her debut?
She wanted to make a big splash.

ANGRY NEIGHBOUR: I'll teach you
to kick footballs into my greenhouse!
NAUGHTY BOY: I wish you would, I
keep missing!

MOTHER: Why are you taking the baby's bib out with you, Tommy? I thought you were going to football practice?

TOMMY: Yes, but the coach said we'd be dribbling this week.

A group of neighbours was organizing a village friendly match followed by a picnic and realized they'd forgotten to invite the eccentric old lady who lived on the green. So they sent a child to invite her. 'It's no use now,' said the old lady, 'I've already prayed for rain.'

What's a dog's favourite
position to play in football?
Golden receiver.

What does a footballer do if
he splits his sides laughing?
Runs until he gets a stitch.

Two boys were trespassing on the local football
pitch when the groundsman came out and
bellowed at them, 'Didn't you see that sign?!'

'Yes, but it said "Private" at the top so we didn't
like to read any further,' replied the boys.

Final Whistle

Why did the football coach go to the theatre?
He wanted to see some great plays.

If you have a referee in
football and an umpire
in cricket, what do you
have in bowls?
Goldfish.

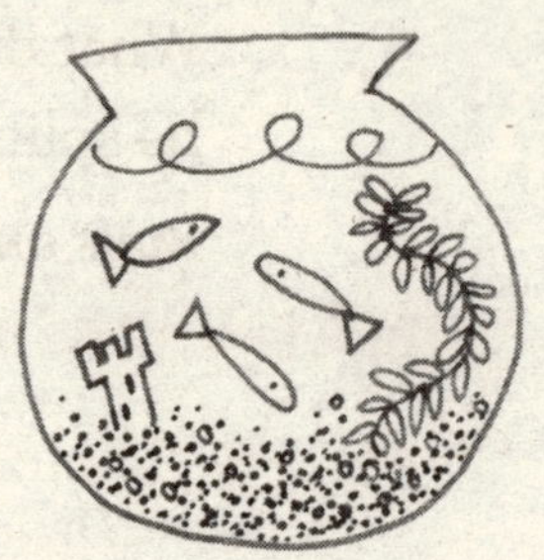

What was the film about referees called?
The Umpire Strikes Back.

Why don't football players make good secret agents?

Because they can't pass without being noticed.

What do you call a referee wearing five balaclavas on a cold day?

Anything you like, he can't hear you.

Who hangs out the washing on a football pitch?

The linesman.

Why did the referee have a sausage stuck behind his ear?

Because he'd eaten his whistle at lunchtime.

A man realized that his new neighbour was a famous football player.

'I've seen you on the TV, on and off,' he said.

'And how do you like me?' asked the player.

'Off,' replied the neighbour.

'Doctor, doctor, come quickly! The referee has swallowed his biro! What can we do?'

'Use another one until I get there.'

A football coach-driver went to a garage.

'Can you have a look at my bus? I think the engine's flooded,' she told the mechanic.

'Is it on the road outside?' asked the mechanic.

'No, it's at the bottom of the canal,' replied the coach-driver.

Why do football players like to tell jokes?
They always score a laugh.

When is a football coach not a football coach?
When it turns into the ground.

JOHN: I've driven a football coach for thirty years and never had an accident.

DON: I guess that makes you a wreck-less driver.

Why was the referee banned from the arena?

For their foul language.

When can a football coach drive on water?

When it goes over a bridge.

CLAUDE: But for Herbert we'd have lost
the match today.

MAUD: Is he the striker or the goalie?

CLAUDE: Neither, he's the ref.

What do you call someone who
stands inside goalposts and
stops the ball rolling away?

Annette.

REFEREE: Will I be able to see
right across the pitch with these
new glasses?

OPTICIAN: Yes.

REFEREE: That's wonderful! I
never could with the old ones.

RACHEL: Three footballers got caught out in the snow, but only two got their hair wet.

LLOYD: Why?

RACHEL: The other one was bald!

Why is a football crowd learning to sing like a person opening a tin of sardines?

They both have trouble with the key.

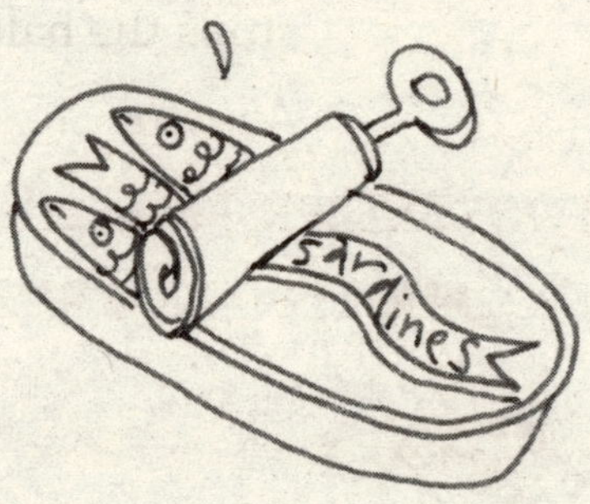

Which part of a football coach is the laziest?

The wheels, they're always tyred.

DAD: Shall I put the kettle on?

SON: You could, but I think you look all right in your football kit.

What ship holds twenty football teams but only three leave it each season?

The Premier-ship!

FOOTBALLER: I didn't come here to be insulted!

DISGRUNTLED FAN: Where do you usually go?

Why are football players good at tests?

Because they always pass.

FATHER TO MUDDY
FOOTBALLING SON: You're
pretty dirty, Bobby.

BOBBY: I'm even prettier clean.

Amelia was speaking about
the opposing team's striker.

'She's out of this world!' he said.

Megan grinned wryly. 'Our team often
wishes she was.'

MILLY: That new striker is a man
who's going places!

WILLY: And the sooner the better!

LEAH: I hear that new player's
mother is an optician.

LEN: Is that why he keeps making
such a spectacle of himself?